Contents

Title page: Cordon bleu, *Uraeginthus bengalus. Front endpapers:* Gold-breasted waxbills, *Amandava subflava. Back endpapers:* Blue-capped waxbills, *Uraeginthus cyanocephala.* Photos by Harry V. Lacey.

Photography:
Elvie and Bates: 24 (top), 35; Robert Gannon: 42 (top); Tom Gardner: 23; Ian Harman: 72; Paul Kwast: 6, 11, 19, 22 (bottom), 26, 30, 74, 75, 78; Harry V. Lacey: 8, 9, 12, 14, 15, 16, 17, 21, 28, 34, 37, 42 (bottom), 55, 57, 58, 62 (top), 67, 68, 73, 82, 85, 86, 88; Mervin F. Roberts: 62 (bottom), 63, 65, 69; Vince Serbin: 38 (bottom); Courtesy of *Tierfreunde:* 71, 90; Louise Van der Meid: 40, 41, 50, 54, 83 (bottom), 91 (top right); Courtesy of Vogelpark Walsrode: 7, 10, 18, 22 (top), 24 (bottom), 27 (top), 31, 49, 66, 70, 79, 83 (top), 87, 91 (top left, bottom).

Acknowledgments

I would like to thank Dr. Val Clear and Jim Plantenga, without whom this book would not have been possible. Also, a special "thank you" to Jenny Smith, to whom this book is dedicated.

ISBN 0-87666-839-2

t.f.h.

Distributed in the U.S. by T.F.H. Publications, Inc., 211 West Sylvania Avenue, PO Box 427, Neptune, NJ 07753; in England by T.F.H. (Gt. Britain) Ltd., 13 Nutley Lane, Reigate, Surrey; in Canada to the pet trade by Rolf C. Hagen Ltd., 3225 Sartelon Street, Montreal 382, Quebec; in Canada to the book trade by H & L Pet Supplies, Inc., 27 Kingston Crescent, Kitchener, Ontario N28 2T6; in Southeast Asia by Y.W. Ong, 9 Lorong 36 Geylang, Singapore 14; in Australia and the South Pacific by Pet Imports Pty. Ltd., P.O. Box 149, Brookvale 2100, N.S.W. Australia; in South Africa by Valid Agencies, P.O. Box 51901, Randburg 2125 South Africa. Published by T.F.H. Publications, Inc., Ltd., the British Crown Colony of Hong Kong.

WAXBILLS

MICHAEL W. GOS

1

(1) Yellow-bellied waxbill, *Estrilda melanotis quartinia.* (2) Black-faced firefinch, *Lagonosticta l. larvata,* male. (3) Peter's twin-spot, *Hypargos neveoguttatus.*

Waxbills are the smallest seed-eating birds and are popular with aviculturists around the world. **Left:** Peter's twin-spot. **Below:** Red-eared waxbills.

What Are Waxbills?

In the bird hobby, this group of birds is called the *waxbill* finches. But there is a problem in defining just what they are. Among aviculturists, the term *finch* generally means any seed-eating bird that is not a hookbill, and waxbills are included with the finches.

In ornithological usage, *waxbill* refers to a relatively large family of birds, the Estrildidae. Of the 124 species, largely of African distribution, most are not spoken of by aviculturists as waxbills. Among these are the common zebra finch, the Java sparrow, and all the mannikins, or nuns.

Purple grenadier, *Uraeginthus ianthinogaster.* The more brightly colored bird is the male.

Rosy twin-spot, *Hypargos margaritatus.* The tan-gray face and breast markings on the female are replaced with dusty red on the male.

10

In two subspecies of the yellow-bellied waxbill, *Estrilda melanotis,* the male has a black face.

Two of the more popular waxbills are (1) red-eared waxbills and (2) cordon-bleus. Both are attractive, sociable birds.

The distinctions between what aviculturists call waxbills and the rest of the finches seem arbitrary, and use of the term *waxbill* varies from person to person, making definition much more difficult. The best that could be stated is very poor. Birds with beaks that look like sealing wax are sometimes called waxbills. However, one of the waxiest bills belongs to the zebra finch. Hobbyists do not classify it as a waxbill, so that characteristic is a poor indicator.

It is nearly impossible, then, to identify waxbills without a great deal of avicultural experience. They are generally four inches or less in length and are seed-eating birds. Beyond that, there is no way to be precise about characteristics.

For the purpose of this book, waxbills will be defined as birds that usually carry the word "waxbill" in their common name or are generally recognized by hobbyists as waxbills. The most common examples are the red-ears, the orange-cheeked, the gold-breasted, the cordon bleu, and the St. Helena.

In general, waxbills are smaller than wrens and possess very active personalities. While none sing, they do emit a cheerful twitter and an interesting cheep. As pets, they are quite manageable because of both their size and their excellent deportment. The individual species are nearly all beautiful in appearance, yet none are really brightly colored. Almost all species are African in origin, with a few being from Asia or Australia.

Hopefully the reader will accept this information and understand that waxbills are what hobbyists choose to call them, and the choice is really arbitrary.

1   2→

(1) Yellow-winged pytilia, *Pytilia hypogrammica*. Being four-and-a-half to five inches long, pytilias are among the larger waxbills. (2) Strawberry finch, *Amandava amandava*. In their native India, males are often kept as songbirds.

Since most waxbills are very adaptable to a variety of conditions, once you have purchased a healthy bird, you should not have much trouble acclimating it in your home. **Left:** Gold-breasted waxbills. **Below:** Melba finch.

Choosing the Bird

Probably the single most important step to successful aviculture is picking the right bird in the first place. Most bird deaths are caused either by exposure to drafts in the home or by diseases that were carried in when the bird was purchased. Fully half the problems can be eliminated simply by getting the right individual initially.

For most hobbyists, there are two ways of procuring new waxbills: either from a breeder or from a petshop. Breeders of waxbills are rare, and virtually all beginners will be obtaining their birds through petshops. With almost no exceptions, waxbills sold in petshops are wild-caught, and

(1) Brown twin-spot, *Clytospiza monteiri.* (2) Dark firefinch, *Lagonosticta rubricata.* (3) Dybowski's twin-spot, *Euchystospiza dybowskii.*

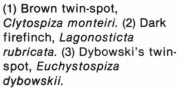

A close relative of the cordon bleu, the blue-breasted waxbill, *Uraeginthus angolensis,* is not so popular because males lack red cheek patches.

their age can vary from newly feathered to elderly. Also, since virtually all are imported, the birds in a shop have recently been through the strictest quarantine procedures in the history of the United States. The current procedures for bird quarantine are much more stringent than those used even for bubonic plague. The typical petshop bird has quite a history behind it.

By law, quarantine stations must be set apart from all other buildings and be within one-half mile of an international airport. In addition, the building must be at least one-half mile from any other poultry. Operation of the station is regulated by the United States Department of Agriculture. Maintaining the health and well-being of the birds is secondary to the main concern: prevention of poultry diseases that may spread to chickens and the like, particularly Exotic Newcastle disease and ornithosis. Unfortunately, if a parrot comes in with Pacheco's disease, the bird is passed and thousands of birds that have been exposed to the disease can later be shipped nationwide. The interests of hobbyists are of no concern.

Each morning, a veterinarian on the USDA staff comes to the quarantine station and unlocks the door, letting in workers. He then locks the door behind them; they must remain in the building all day. The veterinarian then leaves and performs other duties elsewhere, returning at 5 p.m. to let the workers out.

Upon entering the station, workers pass through three rooms. In the first room, clothes are removed and left. In the second room, workers take a disinfectant shower. The third room contains the clothes to be worn for the day's work. Once the clothing change is complete, they will enter into the bird holding rooms to do the day's work.

Air pressure within the quarantine station is less than outside, so all air movement is in, not out. Only filtered air can escape, which guarantees that any disease found in the station will remain there.

Estrilda waxbills come from the grassland areas south of the Sahara in Africa. They are tame birds, and flocks of them are often seen in villages and other areas close to man.

4

(1) Jameson's firefinch, *Lagonosticta rhodopareia jamesonii.* (2,4) Sydney waxbill, *Aegintha temporalis.* (3) Gold-breasted waxbill, *Amandava subflava.*

(1) Black-cheeked waxbills and (2) black-crowned waxbills are not always available in the United States and may be difficult to maintain in good condition.

At the end of each day, everything used during the day is incinerated: paper, clothes, and all wastes. At the end of the thirty-day quarantine period, every bird must either be alive or the veterinarian in charge must have filed a post-mortem report on the dead birds. Should any bird take ill during the quarantine period, it is either treated within the facility or not treated at all. When a death occurs, the post-mortem is done the same day when the veterinarian returns to let the workers out. The examination is done on-premises and the remains are immediately incinerated. If the disease is not communicable to domestic poultry, generally nothing is done. There is no requirement by law for any corrective action on the part of the presiding veterinarian. If because of conscience he chooses to take such action, he may do so, but none is required. If, on the other hand, the disease proves to be communicable to domestic poultry, every bird in the station is destroyed immediately, whether they have the disease or not.

Presumably things occur in the process that may be beneficial to the hobby, but if they do, it is strictly an accidental side effect. It is said that the weak and sickly birds die during this stressful process. As a result, the birds that make it to the shops are supposedly healthy and strong. Whether that is true or not cannot be determined. More likely, even the strong ones are weakened by the whole process.

By the time the bird reaches the petshop, it has suffered through an ordeal that has taken the lives of many of its cagemates and is in a generally weakened state. It is always best to let the bird sit in the shop for ten days to two weeks to be sure there are no latent diseases that manifest themselves due to the bird's weakened condition.

Because waxbills are so small, they possess a very rapid metabolism rate. As a result, any disease that strikes moves through so rapidly that virtually nothing can be done to effect a cure. Knowing this, it is even more vital that the hobbyist find a healthy bird in the first place. Sick birds in the

1

(1) Green avadavat, *Amandava formosa*. (2) Crimson-winged waxbill (aurora finch), *Pytilia phoenicoptera*. (3) Black-faced firefinch, *Lagonosticta l. larvata,* female. (4) Lavender waxbills, *Lagonosticta caerulescens,* and orange-cheeked waxbills, *Estrilda melpoda.*

26

27

Blue-capped waxbills are easy to care for and breed provided they are supplied with a variety of live foods.

hands of experts do not stand much of a chance, and in the hands of an amateur they stand no chance at all. When a hobbyist buys his birds from a petshop, he has no business buying a sick bird.

Fortunately, finding a healthy bird is relatively simple. The following seven-point check, if passed completely, will go far in ensuring the health of the bird. While no check is infallible, most experts agree that the bird that can pass all seven checks is probably going to be healthy.

CHECK #1. Only a sick bird sits fluffed up. It does so when trying to preserve body heat. A bird that sits for extended periods in the fluffed position should never be purchased. Many healthy birds will shake and fluff for a moment, then preen themselves. Such behavior is normal and is the way birds rearrange feathers after being disturbed. It is only when the bird remains fluffed that there is a problem.

CHECK #2. The bird should be active. This is especially the case with waxbills as they are perpetual-motion machines. A waxbill that sits in one position for extended periods of time is not well.

CHECK #3. The bird should not have a messy vent. Again, a bird with this problem should always be avoided. It generally means the bird is having diarrhea, which can be a symptom for dozens of diseases. The messy vent in a healthy bird can also be caused by food problems. However, that is a chance the beginner can ill afford to take. The best way to examine the vent is to take the bird in the hands and examine the under feathers. If the feathers around the vent are soiled, the bird has diarrhea.

CHECK #4. While the bird is still in the hands, gently push the feathers around and examine the skin for external parasites. Not only can they mean problems for the new bird, but they can quickly spread to every other bird in the household. The sight of any pests is a good reason for passing up the bird.

Strawberry finches are hardy birds, easy to breed and care for in captivity. This is a male in courtship display.

(1) Red-faced crimson-wing, *Cryptospiza reichenovii.* (2) Violet-eared waxbill, *Uraeginthus granatina.* (3) Black-crowned waxbill, *Estrilda nonnula.*

CHECK #5. The bird should not be badly plucked. This is not a disease in itself; more likely the bird was the victim of sadistic cagemates. Nevertheless, the bird should not be purchased. A bird with extensive feather plucking is highly susceptible to colds and drafts. In the established household bird, drafts are the single biggest killer. A bird needs all its feathers to combat the ever-present problem.

CHECK #6. Examine the bird for any type of discharge from around the eyes, nose, or mouth. Again symptomatic of a number of maladies, discharge is reason to reject the bird.

CHECK #7. Lastly, check the stool of the bird and its cagemates. Droppings from a waxbill should have a solid dark center with the outer part white and semi-liquid. Any variation from the norm could indicate problems.

For the new hobbyist, it might be a good idea to screen the petshop as well as the birds. The procedure is simple. The buyer should first screen the bird section as a whole. All the cages should be fairly clean and sanitary. The food and water troughs should be both full and clean. If the troughs are soiled with droppings, the birds are probably not receiving proper care. Then examine each of the birds closely, not just the waxbills, but parrots, doves, and the like. Are the birds all healthy looking? This procedure does not have to be as detailed as the examination of particular birds being considered for purchase, but it should include a visual check of each of the birds as they sit in their cages. The birds should be active, alert, and have healthy looking eyes. If the shop passes the test, chances are good that you will be able to find the bird you want in a healthy state.

A good general rule of thumb for waxbills is that any active bird in reasonably good feather is probably a good buy. If the bird of your choice fits that description, then the seven-point check can be applied with an eye toward purchase.

Once the bird is brought home, the acclimation period begins. Fortunately, waxbills are some of the easiest birds to acclimate to a new environment. With the exception of the lavender waxbill, they are mostly hardy birds and take well to new situations. Still, there are a few things the hobbyist can do to make the acclimation period go easier for both the new arrival and for himself.

The biggest risk to birds of any kind is drafts. Birds can catch cold quickly, and birds of waxbill size are particularly sensitive to drafts. The newcomer is under stress as it is. Coupling drafts with the stress is sure to cause problems. As a result, the transport box should always be covered during the trip home. The boxes used by most petshops are adequate for screening out visual stimuli that upset birds, but most are not adequate to prevent blasts of cold air when a car door is opened in winter. A towel over the box will generally be a safeguard in transit.

Once the bird is home, the cage of course should be located in a draft-free area. Waxbills are also subject to heat stroke, so it is a good policy to keep the cage out of direct sunlight as well. With these precautions, any reasonably secure location is fine. Of course, the bird should be protected from frightening stimuli for a while, such as juvenile fingers and grasping cat paws. The bird should be given as much privacy in the beginning as possible. If it is at all possible to provide quiet, that too would be appreciated by nervous birds. A towel placed over the back of the cage will help to rest the bird that is not used to open cages.

After two or three days, the bird should be completely acclimated to its new surroundings. At that point, life should be able to be resumed normally in the vicinity of the cage. The waxbills fit well into normal family life and do not need to be babied. Once they are familiar with the new surroundings, they will thrive even in the rowdiest of households.

Although a large flight or aviary would be ideal housing for waxbills, they can do quite well in cages. **Left:** Gold-breasted waxbills. **Below:** Strawberry finches.

*Care
and
Feeding*

The first step in the care of any bird is the procurement of appropriate housing. Ideally, the hobbyist has an all-glass aviary in his living room or entryway. Unfortunately, most hobbyists do not have such a setup and are forced to settle for a cage. Waxbills are small birds and have special requirements. Though the cage need not be large and several pairs can be kept together, bar spacing is critical. While a budgie cage is more than adequate in size, waxbills would have no problem squeezing between the bars to freedom.

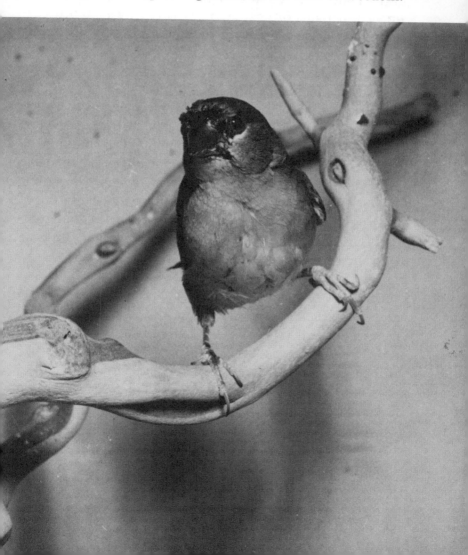

Cages for waxbills should have no openings greater than three-eighths of an inch. Even standard canary cages often fail to hold waxbills.

One consideration in the selection of cages that appears to be simple common sense but is often overlooked is the layout of the cage. The floor should always be the largest dimension of the cage. If the ceiling or any other part above the floor overhangs, the droppings will not remain in the cage. Food and water troughs should never be located under a perch. Fortunately, most cages are designed adequately. It is usually only the ornamental cages designed by companies who know little about birds that are a problem.

Since waxbills are very clean with their droppings, many hobbyists choose not to use the clear plastic or glass sideguards part-way up the cage. The problem is that waxbills are messy with seed hulls. They are not messy like budgies, which throw the hulls around, but the hulls fall to the floor of the cage along with shed feathers. Being active birds, there is always a lot of movement in the cage. Air currents generated by flapping wings blow the debris out of the cage and into the surrounding environment. The solution is to keep these protective sides on the cage in the same way one would with budgies.

One of the beautiful things about waxbills (and finches in general) is that various species can be mixed in a single cage. That makes for a very attractive and colorful display. Many hobbyists try to make the scene even more attractive by adding a beautiful cage. More often than not, that cage will be bamboo or rattan. While the cage is indeed beautiful when new, there are some considerations to be taken into account before purchasing one. When bamboo or rattan cages are soiled, either by droppings or water splashing, they are apt to become stained permanently. It is not long before the once-beautiful cage becomes unsightly. Even more importantly, once wet, the cage tends to attract mites and insect pests that quickly find their way down to the

Various species of waxbills can be housed together or with other bird species. (1) Cordon bleus and firefinch kept with a combassou. (2) Green avadavats with rufous-backed mannikins.

1

WOODEN BIRD TREE 12"

ARBRE 12" EN BOIS POUR OISEAUX

HAGEN

WOODEN SPIRAL BIRD TREE 12"

ARBRE SPIRAL EN BOIS 12" POUR OISEAUX

HAGEN

You can purchase perches (1) and other supplies (2) at your local pet shop—just don't put so many things into the bird cage that it becomes cluttered.

2

BIRD TOYS

skin of the birds. Obviously, prevention is the best cure. While such cages may be beautiful, persons concerned about their pets will find they are really inappropriate.

Cage furnishings are a booming business. There are literally thousands of bird cage furnishings on the market today. Some are necessary, some are useful, and some are absolutely worthless. Among the necessary furnishings are cuttlebone. This product, a dried piece of the skeleton of the cuttlefish (a squid), sharpens and files the bird's beak as it pecks at it. It also supplies calcium and trace elements to the diet.

At the other end of the spectrum are the toys and mirrors commonly seen. While they may have merit in a cage with a single inhabitant, most birds greatly prefer the company of their cagemates, and the toys just get in the way.

Another feature to look for in a cage, or to purchase as an accessory if absent from the chosen cage, is a variety of perch sizes. Waxbills need to be able to hold their feet in different positions from time to time. That is difficult, if not impossible, with the standard dowel rod perch. Ideally, in the largest cages, portions of a tree branch should be provided. In that way the birds have an endless variety of perch sizes all at once. Barring that possibility, the hobbyist should see to it that each perch in the cage is of a different size.

Every two or three days, the cage floor needs to be cleaned and its covering changed. At the same time, any heavy soiling can be removed. Food and water troughs should be thoroughly cleaned. The procedure is rapid, simple, and very necessary to the bird's health. Good hygiene is the best prevention aviculturists have. Regular cleaning will go a long way toward a successful health program.

But once every two weeks, more needs to be done. The entire cage and all of its accessories need to be thoroughly cleaned and disinfected. The best way to accomplish this is by washing everything in a solution of liquid laundry

1

2

(1) Here strawberry finches, zebras and weavers perch on a tree branch suspended from the ceiling. Such natural perches provide your birds with a variety of perch sizes. (2) The bars of this finch cage are spaced so that the birds cannot escape through them. The cage also has been equipped with both natural and store-bought perches.

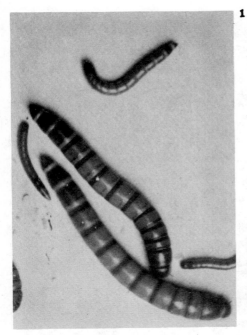

(1) Mealworms are a favorite food of waxbills. (2) The birds enjoying this fresh egg food are yellow-bellied waxbills.

bleach and water. Generally, four ounces of bleach to a gallon of water are sufficient. Stubborn stains can be cleaned with a light brushing, and the remainder of the cage and accessories should either be soaked in the disinfectant solution or washed thoroughly in it. When the cage has dried completely, the birds can be replaced with no ill effects. For aviaries and outdoor cages of large size, the walls and floor can be sprayed with the same formula put into a common garden sprayer. Again, once it is completely dry, the birds can be reintroduced to the cage. This means that some form of alternate, short-term housing is necessary for the birds. Many hobbyists keep the shipping boxes in which the birds were brought home for just that purpose. Others keep a spare cage around just for cleaning day. Regardless of the solution, the process should become an integral part of the bird's care.

In order to move the bird from one cage to another, it must be handled. The hobbyist must be extremely careful in this procedure as the feet and wings of birds this size are extremely fragile and subject to breakage.

Cage location is generally not a problem as long as the guidelines presented earlier are followed. The birds should never be exposed to drafts or forced to sit in direct sunlight. However, a few of the waxbills are a little more delicate and have some special requirements that need to be considered. Gold-breasted, cordon bleu, red-ear, and orange-cheeked waxbills are more delicate and need warmer temperatures than the other waxbills. They are especially susceptible to drafts and need to be in a location well away from doors or leaky windows.

Feeding waxbills is simple, even for beginning aviculturists. They are among the easiest birds in the hobby to feed since the bulk of their diet consists of seeds. Most waxbills will thrive on any good finch mix. In general, finch mixes are mostly millet, and some are exclusively so. There are often a few other types of seeds added to give the

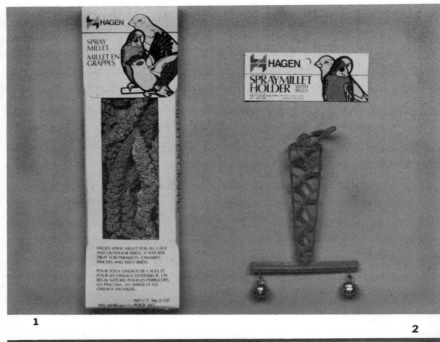

1

2

Millet (1) and various seed mixes made especially for finches (2) will be enthusiastically accepted by waxbills. (3) Many hobbyists supplement the diet of their waxbills with egg food. (4) Many vitamin and food supplements can simply be added to the drinking water.

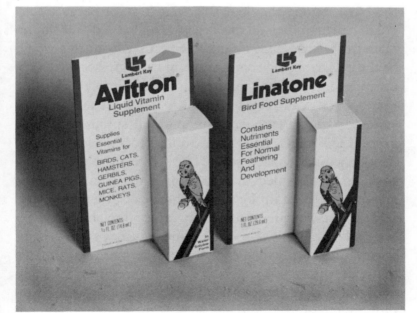

mix color and the hobbyist confidence. Actually, the birds will generally do quite well on straight millet, and some nationally noted hobbyists claim it is difficult to get them to take any other food. Nevertheless, other foods should be offered. It is a practice that should be followed if at all possible, since the healthful gains associated with a varied diet are numerous. The problem here is that waxbills, like all birds, are creatures of habit. They are very slow to change established eating patterns. Some have even been known to starve to death rather than change. It could take as long as three to four weeks of daily offerings before the birds will sample a new food.

Among the foods that should be offered regularly are greens of all types. Lettuce is the poorest of the greens for waxbills, but it will nonetheless supplement the diet well.

Without a doubt, the best green matter supplement is sprouted grass. These are very young grass plants grown for the birds to eat. They can be cultivated in small containers such as jar lids that can later be put into the cage so the birds can eat the greens at their leisure. Because they are live plants, they do not need to be changed and can remain in the cage until eaten. The best seeds for this would be the ryes or a good combination of lawn grasses. Probably the most outstanding mixture can be had simply by sowing some of the wild bird seed sold in petshops and grocery stores. It has an excellent mix and will sprout well. The procedure is much like that used for growing cats' greens, only on a much smaller scale. The seed is merely sown in a small container filled with earth or potting soil. After the grasses have been up for two or three days, they can be offered to the waxbills. As with any other foreign food, waxbills will also be slow to take to this, but they seem to sample it more quickly than any other type of green matter. If a particular pair is slow to sample, sometimes housing them with other birds that do take the grasses will work. Waxbills are imitators, and the objects of their imitation do not necessarily have to be of the same species.

These birds benefit from dietary supplements of fruit as well. Tiny cubes of apples or oranges or half a grape should be offered whenever possible. It is entirely possible that the birds will never sample the fruit, no matter how long it is offered, but it is worth the effort anyway.

One food that nearly every waxbill seems to cherish is live mealworms. Entire cagefuls of birds will descend on a small cup of this food. Mealworms are usually available from most larger petshops and can be raised by the hobbyist if necessary.

Besides millet, there is one other food that is vital and should always be fed. Waxbills seem to require more protein than the zebras or other finches. As a result, they need a protein supplement. Several good supplements suitable for birds and enjoyable to waxbills are available at your pet dealer. Most can be served in a finger cup to an entire cageful of birds at a time.

There are many places where food for waxbills can be purchased. It is always a good policy to get it from a petshop, unless you are a large-scale hobbyist who buys in bulk. Petshops usually buy their seed in bulk wherever they can get the best price. Regardless of price, most shop owners make sure it is a good mixture, because the reputation of their business depends on it.

Many hobbyists feel an egg supplement is essential to waxbills, especially during breeding time. Most petshops carry egg biscuits designed specifically for this purpose.

Like all birds, the waxbills will also need drinking and bathing water. It is wise to keep the two separate, as bathing water tends to become soiled quickly with droppings. The small water bowls built into the cage walls are good for drinking water, while a small tray such as a foil potpie pan works well for bathing. Neither the drinking nor the bathing water needs to be warmed for waxbills, despite the small size of these birds.

Left: Cuttlebone should always be available to your birds. It provides nutrients and helps to keep birds' beaks in good condition.
Below: A pair of Peter's twin-spots in a cage in which heat can be applied from below.

Diseases
of
Waxbills

Generally, waxbills are very hardy, manageable birds. It is a good thing that this is the case since their tiny size makes them very difficult to cure once disease has struck. While they suffer from few diseases, there are enough problems to cause a certain in-shop motality rate. The price of waxbills has much to do with their delicate nature, which is due to size. The hardiness develops once the birds are situated in the home, but prior to that time they are less-

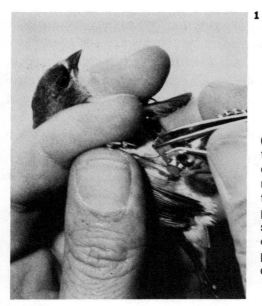

(1) Here a strawberry finch is getting its overgrown claws trimmed. (2) These finches have feather problems. (3, 4) Pet shops have a variety of health-related products for the care of your birds.

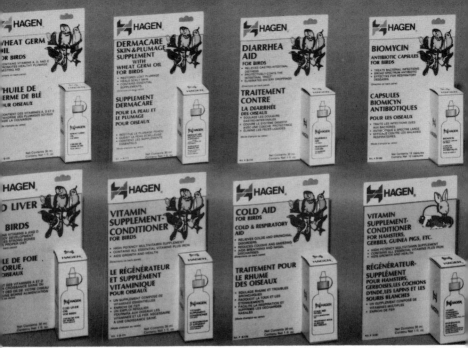

3

4

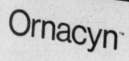

Ornacyn™

Treatment for
respiratory diseases
of pet birds

Broad spectrum antibiotic
(erythromycin) capsules
for birds' drinking water

 Mardel
Laboratories, Inc.

Contents 8 Capsules

Net Wt. 2 Grams

than-sturdy animals. Even though a waxbill costs very little if you're buying it in Africa, the costs of transportation, feeding during quarantine, and quarantine station operation cause the price to rise. Coupling this with the increased mortality that results from the extended in-transit period means that by the time that African waxbill reaches your petshop it is an expensive bird.

As was mentioned before, the reason for the quarantine procedure is to prevent the introduction of Exotic Newcastle disease and ornithosis. Should either of these get by the quarantine station, the hobbyist can expect them to show up immediately or not at all. They are not diseases that a family pet will develop two years down the road unless it is exposed to another bird infected with the disease at that time. The chances of the diseases getting past the quarantine stations to begin with are miniscule.

One of the problems faced by waxbill enthusiasts is the lack of professional help when it comes to diseases. Few veterinarians today have received training in birds. However, when it comes to waxbills, it makes little difference. While an experienced veterinarian may be able to identify the disease after the fact (that is, after death), often nothing can be done to save the life of an ailing bird. The metabolism of waxbills is so high that some diseases will just race to climax in a matter of hours or less. Sometimes the bird is dead just minutes after showing symptoms.

There are a few products on the market that are used medicinally for birds, including wide-spectrum antibiotics. Since they may or may not be helpful for birds as small as a waxbill, get the advice of your dealer. But keep in mind that the efficacy of any medication can only be judged in relation to a specific incidence of disease in a particular bird.

One procedure has helped in the treatment of ailing waxbills, and it can be administered as easily by a hobbyist as by a veterinarian. A treatment for any disease, then, is application of heat. The procedure is simple: a forty-watt light bulb is placed next to the cage and turned on. A large towel is then placed over the light and the cage, throwing the bulb's heat directly to the bird. (Be careful to keep the towel away from the bulb.) The sick bird should receive this heat treatment for a full twenty-four hours. At the end of that time, the bulb can be turned off but the towel should remain in place for another two to three hours to allow the heat to dissipate slowly and prevent chilling the bird. In most cases, if any treatment is successful, this one is it.

As is the case with any animal, prevention is the best policy where the health of waxbills is concerned. A few commonsense precautions will go a long way toward maintaining the birds' health. Waxbills are most susceptible to cold. Nearly all diseases can be prevented simply by keeping the birds in a warm, draft-free place. The "warm" part is much less important than the "draft-free." Waxbills can generate enough heat and hold it within their feathers for self-protection provided none of it is taken away by drafts. Most waxbills can withstand temperatures as low as 55°F. for prolonged periods. A bird left in a breezy place will more than likely become ill in a matter of hours. For that reason, great care should be exercised in choosing the location for the cage.

Food and water troughs need to be kept as clean and sanitary as possible. In addition to the disinfecting process described earlier, it is important that the food and water troughs never be located under perches. To do otherwise is an open invitation to disease. Regular cleaning and disinfecting of all items that come in contact with the birds will go a long way toward ensuring a long and healthy life for the waxbills.

In spite of drawbacks because of their small size, waxbills are with few exceptions hardy birds. They are a good beginner's bird and can be successfully maintained with little or no prior experience in aviculture.

If you do not want to take the chance of cross-breeding among your birds, true pairs should be placed in separate cages. **Left:** Cordon bleu, zebra, strawberry, and red-eared waxbill. **Below:** A pair of gold-breasted waxbills.

Breeding Waxbills

Breeding waxbills is not a subject that can be taken lightly. Frankly, they are not easy birds to breed. While many hobbyists are able to get their birds to produce eggs on a regular basis, getting those eggs hatched and the young raised is not an easy task. For that reason, virtually all pet-shop waxbills are wild-caught. Occasionally cage-bred birds are available from breeders, but they command higher prices. The theory is that cage-bred birds are more likely to breed in captivity than are their wild-caught counterparts. Whether that is true or not, the prices for domestically raised waxbills are high.

While waxbill young are hard to produce and even harder to raise in captivity, breeding and raising success can be enhanced when the birds are kept in a planted aviary. There are several reasons why this is the case. The plants provide some degree of shelter and privacy required by the birds. There are some species that will abandon a nest of eggs if they are disturbed in any way. Also, the small insects so vital to the raising of the young are usually more available in the planted aviary, especially if it is outdoors in a warm area. The best plantings for persons interested in raising waxbills are low bushes. These small birds like to build their nests close to the ground in areas with good foliage cover.

Of course, the most obvious requirement in any attempt to breed birds is the presence of a true pair, male and female. While this is an apparently obvious requirement, many beginning hobbyists overlook that fact because they readily assume that what the petshop sells as a pair is just that. That is not always the case. In some species the sexes are indistinguishable. There are only two factors that give the hobbyist even a hint at which sex is which. Generally the cocks are more brightly colored than the hens. However, unless you can select from a group of ten, taking the most and least brightly colored individuals, that may not help much either. The only sure difference is in the behavior of the males. When a bird is seen doing a strange dance while singing, it can be safely assumed the bird is male. Unfortunately, this behavior is usually shown only at breeding times and will probably not be available as a guide when purchasing the birds.

The best method of determining pairs is the group selection method. It is expensive unless the breeder of cage-bred birds has already performed the service for you. The procedure involves placing five or more birds of the same species into a cage, each bird with a different distinguishing mark. Some breeders use differently colored leg bands,

For those species which are hard to sex, put several birds together and let them pair off naturally. Shown here is a group of blue-breasted waxbills.

(1) A pair of green avadavats. (2) A pair of strawberry finches, also called red avadavats.

while others make marks on different body areas with Mercurochrome or a felt pen. A single mark is made on the chest of one bird, the wing of another, the leg of another, and so on. The birds are then allowed to pair off naturally. When any pair shows signs of breeding behavior, they can be identified and removed. This is done by noting either the band color or the location of the body mark. It can usually be assumed that birds pairing off this way are true pairs. One word of caution is necessary, though. In the rare case where all birds in the cage are male, two males will occasionally court each other. As a result, there are no absolute guarantees.

For persons of less financial freedom, buying three birds will increase the possibilities of obtaining a pair. It should be noted that not only does the group selection method increase chances of getting a pair, but it also has the advantage of allowing the birds to choose their own mates. That enhances the possibility of a completed breeding cycle later on. Most animals prefer to pick their own mates, and waxbills are no exception.

In spite of the many advantages of planted outdoor aviaries, most hobbyists will attempt to breed these birds in small indoor cages. They can be and are bred in this manner regularly by many hobbyists. Nevertheless, it is difficult.

Waxbills prefer to breed in a closed nest. The open nests used by so many birds lack the security, privacy, and protection that waxbills crave. As was mentioned before, mere interference can cause these shy birds to abandon their nests totally.

The best nesting system seems to be the use of 1½-pint plastic freezer boxes of a cubic shape. These are roughly four inches on a side. With the lid firmly fastened, cut out half the bottom. The box is then placed on end with the cut section of the bottom in the air. This can either be placed directly into the cage on the floor or can be mounted against an outside wall with an opening allowing the birds to leave the cage to enter the nest box.

Once the box is in place, the birds prefer to do their own nest-building. It is up to the hobbyist to provide the appropriate nesting material. The best substance for waxbills seems to be burlap. Burlap bags can be cut into three-inch-square segments and then pulled apart into individual threads. It is important that the segments be no longer than three inches. Longer threads can cause the accidental hanging of a bird. For persons with less time, any store-bought nesting material will do. Most petshops carry products suitable for waxbills.

In any circumstances, it is imperative that acrylic yarn be avoided. One of the nation's leading bird enthusiasts, Dr. Val Clear, tells of how the legs on a half dozen birds were lost due to the use of acrylic yarn. Upon checking one of the bird's legs with a magnifying glass, he saw tiny filaments of the yarn wrapped tightly around them. These filaments would keep getting tighter until circulation was cut off and the legs were lost. While burlap may be more difficult to prepare and store-bought nesting material may be more expensive, in the long run acrylic yarn can cause more trouble and expense than either of the alternative substances and should never be used.

When waxbills are breeding, and even more when raising young, they need special foods that really aren't required in the everyday diet. One of these is a good egg food. This should be offered as a dietary supplement as soon as a pair of birds begins to nest. Most petshops can provide a commercially prepared egg biscuit suitable for waxbills. This should be served in small amounts so there is always some available to the birds. Change the feed twice daily to prevent spoilage. Along with the egg mix, the birds should receive all the greens they care to eat. Most waxbills will consume more greens during the breeding process.

After the young hatch, it is even more imperative to use

the egg mixture regularly. Parent waxbills feed the mixture to their young directly, so consumption of it will increase.

Another necessity in breeding is additional protein, particularly in the form of live insects. In the planted aviary outdoors, the birds can pretty much fend for themselves. Indoors, the mealworms that they should normally be offered will usually be sufficient, but any other small insects will be appreciated. Many petshops feed their birds old fish food that has become "buggy." While it is the insects that the birds are after, a few bites of high-quality fish food can only be beneficial to their health.

The courtship rituals in waxbills are interesting and entertaining. It is precisely this behavior which makes it possible to sex the birds. During the breeding period, the males suddenly become quite territorial. Normally six or eight birds will sleep in the same nesting box, but when breeding begins, this practice usually ceases.

Often the first sign of breeding which the hobbyist will notice is the male's dance. It is quite unique, and the bird puts everything into the movements. The procedure begins with the male spreading his feathers in all directions, much like a porcupine does its quills. This gives him the appearance of a much larger bird. He will then move right in front of the female and begin prancing up and down on the perch in an awkward position. He raises and lowers his body by bending his legs. Sometimes these movements become so vigorous that the bird actually leaves the perch and begins jumping up and down. The head arches back, thrusting the chest forward, and he utters a bit of a song. All the while the object of his interest, in her inimitable way, ignores him. Eventually she does show some interest and they make their way to the nest.

After the mating takes place, both the male and the female work on building the nest. When the nest is complete, the hen enters and lays the eggs. The average incubation period for waxbills is fourteen days. When the pea-

1

2

Waxbills prefer nests which offer privacy and protection, and although a cube-shaped nest box (1) seems to be ideal, other types could also be provided so that the birds can make their own choice. (2) A basket nest which has been lined with feathers. (3) The two cleaned halves of this coconut shell are held together with a rubber band.

sized eggs hatch, the parents begin the rearing process. The young will stay in the nest for two more weeks, being fed by the parents all the while. At the end of that time, they will begin to venture out into the world. After they leave the nest, the parents will still feed them for another two weeks.

As soon as the young birds begin to eat millet or any other hard seed on their own, they should be removed from the cage. Should the male re-enter breeding condition after weaning, he will become aggressive toward them. The young can be safely moved once they have started feeding themselves on their own.

Often a pair of waxbills will lay a clutch of eggs and then abandon them. There may be several reasons for such behavior, one of which is a bird's uncanny ability to tell when the eggs are bad. But in some cases the birds simply abandon perfectly fertile eggs. Other pairs may carry the process to the point of hatching out young and then abandon them, leaving them to die. Because of the small size of the young, hand-rearing is not practical with waxbills. At best, such procedures are a monumental pain and are often shunned by hobbyists even with the nestlings of larger birds. With waxbills it is next to impossible. Even hand-rearing will not help if the birds abandon the nest before hatching. Fortunately, waxbill eggs can be fostered to other bird quite easily, a procedure that is really quite common among breeders.

Society (Bengalese) finches are the prime candidates for use in fostering, as some will incubate and raise any small finch (including waxbills). Fostering also has the added advantage of getting more young from a pair of laying birds. Once the eggs are taken from the nest, the breeding process begins again, and more eggs can be generated in the time otherwise required for hatching and rearing.

The fostering procedure is simple. A pair of foster parents is allowed to breed and lay a clutch of eggs. At the same time, the waxbills are doing the same thing. After the

Covered nest baskets, whether of coarse (1) or fine (2) wicker approximate the kind of nest structures waxbills build in the wild.

1

4→

(1) Dusky twin-spot, *Euchystospiza cinereovinacea.* (2) Fawn-breasted waxbill, *Estrilda paludicola.* (3) Bar-breasted firefinch, *Lagonosticta rufopicta.* (4) St. Helena waxbill, *Estrilda astrild.*

2

3

2

(1) Society finches, also known as Bengalese finches, can be used as foster-parents of young waxbills. (2) A society finch brooding.

clutch is complete, the waxbills will begin sitting or will abandon the nest, while the foster parents tend their own clutch. At this point the breeder takes the waxbill eggs and puts them under the foster hen. He then has the option of discarding the foster hen's own eggs or leaving them there to incubate as well. Since the feeding demands of so many young may be a problem later, most breeders choose to dispose of the original eggs. The foster hen then raises the waxbill eggs as her own. The young are reared successfully and the parents never seem to wonder why junior looks so different from mom and dad.

While the procedures are rather simple and straightforward, getting the birds to cooperate is an entirely different matter. There are so many places where a pair of birds can sabotage the procedure that breeding waxbills successfully is very difficult. The problems are compounded when the species selected is an especially tough breeder, such as the lavender waxbill. With persistence and patience it can be done, especially if the hobbyist is willing to give fostering a try.

←—1

2

(1) Schlegel's green-backed twin-spot, *Mandingoa nitidula schlegeli,* is the prettiest race of green-backed twin-spots. (2) Red-billed firefinch, *Lagonosticta senegala,* is the most commonly available firefinch. .

Waxbills and birds of the genus *Lonchura* are frequently housed together in mixed collections. **Left:** Chestnut-breasted mannikin, *L. castaneothorax.* **Below:** Indian silverbills, *L. malabarica,* and pearl-headed silverbills, *L. caniceps.*

Species

While there is much confusion in the hobby as to which birds are waxbills, there are certain birds universally accepted by ornithologists and hobbyists alike as being waxbills. In this chapter I will deal with the most popular species of waxbills in America today. There are several other species that will not be covered due to their extremely high cost or unavailability. Also, those common birds classified as waxbills only by ornithologists and not by aviculturists are omitted as well. What follows below is an

St. Helena waxbills, *Estrilda astrild*, the largest of the *Estrilda* waxbills. That this is a male is evidenced by the intensity of the red markings.

Red-eared waxbill, *Estrilda troglodytes,* one of the smaller *Estrilda* waxbills. Distinguishing the sexes is not easy, so if breeding is desired more than one pair should be purchased.

outline of the birds the reader is likely to find in his pet-shop.

RED-EARED WAXBILL

The red-eared waxbill, *Estrilda troglodytes,* is very similar in appearance to the St. Helena waxbill, *Estrilda astrild.* The body is a basic grayish brown color all over, with perhaps more gray on the underside. The name comes from the deep maroon-red stripe that runs over each eye from the beak to the eye and slightly beyond. It is one of the smallest of the common waxbills, measuring less than four inches, including the tail. Because the red-ear has been imported for a long time, one would expect the price to be low and the bird to be heavily bred domestically. Neither is the case. The price of the red-ear is much the same as the rest of the common waxbills. Like most other waxbills, breeding is difficult and most specimens bought in this country are still wild-caught birds.

Red-ears are very shy birds and are never really tame although they do occasionally get used to their owner and become more comfortable in his presence. Most red-ears, especially in the early days in a new home, will not even feed in the presence of the owner or other human intruders.

ST. HELENA WAXBILL

The St. Helena, *Estrilda astrild,* is without a doubt one of the best waxbills for the beginning hobbyist. They are extremely hardy birds and are good candidates for the hobbyist who has an eye toward breeding. Looking much like the red-ear, the St. Helena is larger, any barring more pronounced, and belly and undertail coverts black. Found on much of the African continent and the surrounding islands, this bird possesses a very amusing personality. In addition to being constantly in motion like the rest of its family, the St. Helena has a propensity for hanging upside down from the cage wires or suspended millet sprays. It then spreads its tail feathers like a fan and wags the tail from side to side.

Many St. Helena owners claim that the bird will not stop breeding once the process starts. That does not indicate that starting the process is simple, however. The hen generally lays four eggs and is quite aggressive in their defense. Twelve days to two weeks later, the eggs hatch after being tended predominantly by the female. The parents tend the young in the nest for three weeks more after hatching.

ORANGE-CHEEKED WAXBILL

Another good beginner's waxbill is the orange-cheeked, *Estrilda melpoda*. This little bird is distinguished from the two preceding species: the eye stripe is absent, but cheek patches are a vivid orange. It is very hardy, particularly with regard to temperature variations. Although keeping orange-cheeked waxbills may be relatively simple, breeding them is another matter. To begin with, the sexes are nearly impossible to differentiate. As if that weren't enough, the birds simply show a lack of interest in the whole process of breeding. Should the process begin at all, it is a casual, slipshod affair with the nest being poor to non-existent. It is no wonder so few hobbyists have been able to breed the bird. There are reports of breeding activities that culminate in the hatching of young but stop when the parents refuse to tend to feeding chores. Many feel this is due to the absence of appropriate live foods for feeding the hatchlings. Regardless of the reason, all these factors make the orange-cheeked waxbill a difficult bird to breed.

CORDON BLEU

One of the more frequently available common waxbills is the cordon bleu, *Uraeginthus bengalus*. Because it is less hardy than other family members, the cordon bleu is subject to greater shipping and quarantine losses. Once the bird is in the home, special care should be taken in the acclimation

Lavender waxbills, also known as lavender finches, are natives of West Africa. As they are highly insectivorous, they should be provided with live food, especially if good breeding results are desired.

(1) Lavender waxbill, *Lagonosticta caerulescens.* (2) Orange-cheeked waxbill, *Estrilda melpoda.* (3) Chubb's green-backed twin-spot, *Mandingoa nitidula chubbi.*

period. Temperatures should not be allowed to go below 65°F., and drafts and dampness must be avoided.

Cordon bleus should have a supplemental insect diet, but many are slow to try new food, especially if it is not of the live variety. A good way to get the new birds to sample the insect matter is to cage them with other finches that are already eating the food. Bleus tend to imitate the behavior of their cagemates, regardless of species. For the more enterprising hobbyists, the wingless variety of *Drosophila*, the fruit fly, is a perfect food, and most cordon bleus take it immediately.

Generally, cordon bleus are not good breeders, but an occasional pair will become prolific. The traditional waxbill courtship dance is slightly different in this species. When jumping up and down in front of the female, the male cordon bleu drops his wings for added show.

Four eggs are usually laid, sometimes more. The nest is built by both birds, but the male never shares in the incubation. Instead, he takes a protective guarding position outside the nesting box when his mate is away. All during the breeding season the male is short-tempered.

Another problem that makes cordon bleus tough to breed is their tendency to abandon the nest at the slightest disturbance. The male will make a token effort to turn back the intruder, but failing that, he and the hen will leave the nest permanently.

The young hatch in thirteen days, and then the search by the parents for the appropriate live food is on. They need small insects, and even for the chicks, *Drosophila* seems to be the best bet. The parents will partially pre-digest the food, so size is not really important. The young remain in the nest fourteen to eighteen days and are fed up to a week and a half after leaving the nest. After that time, they should be removed in case the male re-enters breeding condition. Should he do so, he will begin to persecute his young.

LAVENDER WAXBILL

The lavender waxbill, *Lagonosticta caerulescens,* is probably the poorest choice of the common waxbills for beginners. The bird is simply not hardy enough for the novice to take a chance with. The name is a complete misnomer, as the body is gray and the tail a deep red. At no time in its life cycle does this bird ever assume a lavender color.

Lavenders are fairly large birds as waxbills go, but they are friendly to other birds nonetheless. Even if there are several lavenders together and they are not getting along, they will still all sit shoulder to shoulder on the same perch.

A problem with lavenders is that they tend to be feather-pluckers. This is particularly the case with males.

Lavenders are very difficult birds to breed. In those rare times when a pair had laid eggs, the clutch was immediately abandoned. Should the hobbyist have a pair of lavenders lay, it is strongly recommended that the eggs be fostered immediately. Just be sure that the foster parents will feed insect matter or the young will not survive.

CRIMSON-WINGED WAXBILL

The crimson-winged waxbill, *Pytilia phoenicoptera,* comes from the Senegal region of Africa and is less popular than the previously discussed birds. Also known as the aurora finch, this bird has a basically black body covered with a pearly white scaling that resembles tiny teardrops.

Crimson-wings acclimate to new environments easily and settle down rather quickly, although they never really get tame. They are a larger bird than most of the waxbills but are not really bullies.

One positive point in the case of the crimson-winged is the willingness to breed. If the bird is moved to an outdoor aviary, the breeding process can start in just a matter of days. It can be several more days before the cock gets the hen interested enough to join him in his nest-building tasks.

Gold-breasted waxbills are tame birds, often seen in flocks near cultivated and grassland areas south of the Sahara in Africa. They acclimate well to aviary or cage life.

(1) Neuman's waxbill, *Lagonosticta thomensis.* (2) The nominate subspecies of the yellow-bellied waxbill, *Estrilda melanotis.*

The normal laying consists of four to six eggs that are rather elongated. For the next two weeks, both birds take turns sitting on the eggs, with the female doing the job throughout the night. Fortunately, adult crimson-wings will feed the young anything available, although they greatly prefer small insect matter. Unfortunately, that is where the easy part ends. For some reason, raising the young is not an often-accomplished task. The reasons for this are yet unknown, but hopefully the problem will be solved in the future.

Hobbyists keeping crimson-winged waxbills should pay special attention to providing sprouted grasses, as this bird shows a definite need for green matter and does not seem fond of lettuce and the like.

GOLD-BREASTED WAXBILL

This is the smallest (2½ inches) of the waxbills commonly imported. Of course, its width is correspondingly small, and that spells trouble. It takes a special cage to hold a pair of gold-breasted waxbills, *Amandava subflava,* as they slide between the bars of most cages with no trouble at all. No hole in the cage should exceed three-eighths inch in width or the birds are gone.

This bird, also called the orange-breasted waxbill, get along well with other small birds, including its own kind. The name comes from the bright orange chest sported by the male of the species. The female's buff chest has just a hint of orange. Breeding this species seems fairly easy, but like the crimson-winged, raising the young is not something often done successfully.

OTHER WAXBILLS

There are several other species of waxbills that are occasionally seen in petshops, but they tend to be rare. One is the strawberry finch, or red avadavat, *Amandava amandava.* It gets its name from the bright red courtship colors

(1) Tri-colored man-nikins, Lonchura malacca, are regularly imported and are attractive cagemates for waxbills. (2) Though not as finely colored as the tri-coloreds, black-headed mannikins, *Lonchura atricapilla,* and white-headed mannikins, *Lonchura maja,* can also be housed with waxbills.

(1,3) Melba finch, *Pytilia melba.* (2) Orange-winged pytilia, *Pytilia afra.* The male melba finch is more brightly colored than the female.

87

**1**

(1) Chestnut-breasted mannikin, *Lonchura castaneothorax.* (2) Bronze-winged mannikin, *Lonchura cucullata.* During the breeding season, bronze-wingeds can be very aggressive toward other small birds and so should be housed alone or, if kept with waxbills, in a very roomy aviary.

2

of the male. Unfortunately the female (and the male when not in breeding condition) is rather gray. This is a good beginner's bird when available, as it is extremely hardy. The only problem one would encounter with this species is that the cock will be aggressive toward others of his own species during breeding season.

The fire finch, *Lagonosticta senegala,* is a tough bird to keep because of its need for live food. Of course, that need also means the price will be much higher, as costs of keeping the birds through shipping and quarantine periods are high. When purchasing one of these birds, be sure that it is eating. Often the eating reflex ceases in the trauma associated with shipping. That is also coupled with the fact that very few of them receive the necessary live foods throughout the shipping and quarantine ordeal.

Of course, occasionally the hobbyist may run across other waxbills not covered here. In general, where there is not much information to be had, the best advice would be to check with the shop owner. Often on a rare shipment he will receive some information on the birds and can pass it on to the buyer. In any case, giving the rare bird the optimum care described in this book will do much toward ensuring the bird's well-being.

1

(1) Cordon bleu, *Uraeginthus bengalus.*
(2) Yellow-winged pytilia, *Pytilia hypogrammica.* (3) Black-cheeked waxbill, *Estrilda erythronotos.* (4) Blue-capped waxbill, *Uraeginthus cyanocephala.* (5) Black-tailed lavender finch, *Lagonosticta perreini.*

2

3

4

5

Waxbills are charming, attractive small birds, ideal for the beginning aviculturist. **Left:** A small mixed collection of waxbills. **Below:** This colorful bird collection includes weavers, society finches, spice finches, zebra finches and strawberry finches.

In Closing

Waxbills are a group of beautiful little birds that will brighten any home. Unless breeding is the object, let me suggest that the hobbyist consider large cages with several different species. Perhaps even a mixture of waxbills and other finch-type birds will be considered. These colorful little birds can do much to add beauty and charm. Because species can be mixed, the cage will always be exciting with the many colors and the absolutely fascinating antics of the waxbills.

A good beginner's bird in many cases, a waxbill is to be recommended to anyone with an interest in aviculture. The prices are very reasonable, and the pleasure they give when well cared for is endless.